410-308-2583

God Loves You Better Than Mac And Cheese

Helen McLeod Rogers

WestBow
PRESS
A DIVISION OF THOMAS NELSON

Copyright © 2012 Helen McLeod Rogers

All rights reserved. No part of this book may be used or reproduced by any means, graphic, electronic, or mechanical, including photocopying, recording, taping or by any information storage retrieval system without the written permission of the publisher except in the case of brief quotations embodied in critical articles and reviews.

WestBow Press books may be ordered through booksellers or by contacting:

WestBow Press
A Division of Thomas Nelson
1663 Liberty Drive
Bloomington, IN 47403
www.westbowpress.com
1-(866) 928-1240

Because of the dynamic nature of the Internet, any web addresses or links contained in this book may have changed since publication and may no longer be valid. The views expressed in this work are solely those of the author and do not necessarily reflect the views of the publisher, and the publisher hereby disclaims any responsibility for them.

Any people depicted in stock imagery provided by Thinkstock are models, and such images are being used for illustrative purposes only.

Certain stock imagery © Thinkstock.

ISBN: 978-1-4497-6004-5 (sc)
ISBN: 978-1-4497-6006-9 (hc)
ISBN: 978-1-4497-6005-2 (e)

Library of Congress Control Number: 2012912854

Printed in the United States of America

WestBow Press rev. date: 08/09/2012

Thank you to my wonderful husband who loves me and gets me to all my speaking engagements. He is my EPS (Ed Positioning System).

This book is for my precious children Marsha, Dawn, Tom, Tim, Jeff and Susie. I love you precious grandchildren: Heidi, Kassi, and Cole, Sean and Ericka, you are miracles from God.

To my sweet sisters, Marilyn and Sue and to our parents who are with Jesus.

Thank you Jesus for being my Lord and Savior; for allowing me to be your child and work in your kingdom.

Contents

"Not Him Lord" 1
Bucket of Blessings. 5
Mount Diaper 7
Special Delivery 9
From Death to Life 11
Yvonne. 15
Heidi 17
Heart's Desire 21
Love is Color-Blind 23
God Speaks Chinese. 25
One Baby's Worth 27
God's Box 29
Money from Heaven. .31
Seven Abortions 33
Seeing with God's eyes. 35
The Greatest Gift 37
Precious Memories. 39
Heavenly Haircut 41
The Nightmare. 43
Hope 45
Amy's Miracle 47
The Not So Good Abraham 49
Diapers from Heaven 51
Sue's Story 53
Cole 55

The Eyes of a Child 57
Katie's Story 59
A Friend's Story 61
The Double Sunflower 63
Chloe 65
Show Me My Baby. 67
Kassi. 69
What I Learned On The Farm 71
Macaroni and Cheese 73
Never Tell Dad 75
Zucchini 77
The Dead Cat. 79
Tim and the Tape 81
The Truck. 83
The Turkey 85
My Baptism. 87
Dawn's Graduation. 89
Mission Home 91
Pray for Me 93
The Dream 95
Money Hunt 97
God is Calling 99
Poochie and the Snake. 101
Are You a Dandelion? 103
The Man on the Cadillac 105
Together Forever. 107
A Blessing. 109
Tommy 111
Neal 113
The Doughnut Prayer 115
I Aborted Three Children. 117
The Atheist 119
The Homeless 121
Daddy and Me 123
Ms. Halley 125

Bill 127
"Modern Day" Proverbs Women 129
The Job 131
Mom. 133
Math Teacher of the Year 135
Jesus With Skin On 137
I Needed A Dad 139
Author. 141

These stories are true but the names and places are changed to protect our clients.

"Not Him Lord"

"For I know the thoughts that I think toward you, saith the Lord, thoughts of peace, and not of evil, to give you an unexpected end." Jeremiah 29:11-13 (KJV)

I saw an abortion on television around 23 years ago and it made me very angry. The "red-head" temper in me wanted to punch somebody for killing God's precious babies. I believe the womb is supposed to be the safest place on earth for a baby. I wondered what has happened to us as human beings that we would kill our own children for the sake of convenience. I went to God in prayer and He assured me that He had a better way to fight this attack on life. I saw a flyer for a life ministry in Rocky Mount that was conducting a volunteer training. My intentions were to volunteer in the clothing closet since I was too shy to become a counselor.

On Saturday, I was at the center and the main counselor called in and she was sick. I remember standing at the crisis pregnancy center door praying that no one would show up as I did not feel prepared to counsel. God's answer to that prayer was, "I have a divine appointment for you today. You are my handmaiden and I am in control. Now, pray, Lord, whoever you want to send today, we are ready."

Ten minutes later, a large man on his Harley motorcycle rode up in front of the center. I looked at this man. He was dressed in black leather, black boots, long stringy hair, gold chains around his neck, and tattoos everywhere.

On the back of the motorcycle sat a 15 year old girl. I prayed, "Dear God, please send this man to the shoe store next door." God said, "No!" That big man walked into the center, he never said a word, and pushed the teenager toward me. She said, "Miss, I need a pregnancy test, I think I'm pregnant." I looked at the big man and felt afraid. I quickly took the girl to the counseling room. We did a pregnancy test and the test was negative. This gave me an opportunity to share God's love for her and His plans for her life. We talked about second virginity and that she was precious to God. She accepted Jesus that day. After she accepted Jesus, she asked me to please tell her Daddy the things I had shared with her. I agreed to tell him and told her to bring him to the center.

She turned to me and said, "He's in the waiting room." I cringed at the thought of sharing with this man. I even asked God if He knew this man was her father. God knew and reminded me that he had a plan for this encounter. I asked the man into the counseling room, my thoughts were running wild. "God, this is a really big scary man. He looks like he could hurt me, he may not listen."

I prayed, "Lord, this is all yours." Since I am a kindergarten teacher of 38 years, I have learned to talk fast because kindergarten children have very short attention span. Remember this man had not said a word the entire time. I shared as quickly as I could. The man never moved or spoke, he just sat there. I finished what I thought God wanted me to say. I felt good about things so far. Then God said, "Ask him if you can pray for him?" I told God I didn't know if this man knew much about prayer. "Have you seen this man?" was my question to God.

You see I was judging and that was a sin. God's reply was "I made him and I died for him, who made you judge?" My answer to God was "Yes, Lord, and I ask you to forgive me for judging." I asked the man if I could pray for him. The man nodded, he never said a word, he stood, took my hand and his daughter's hand. We formed a circle in that room that day. I felt like the Bible story of the three men in the furnace and the fourth was like unto the Son of God.

God did come into that room that day and spoke to each one of us personally. He reminded me that I am not to judge others. The teenager was reminded not to get ahead of God's plans for her life. She was to stay abstinent and wait on the Lord. I did not know what the Lord was saying to the father. I finished the prayer.

As the man started to leave, he turned to me, and took my hand and said, "Thank you, Lady, you see my wife left me this week, I thought my 15 year old daughter was pregnant, I lost my job, and I was thinking about committing suicide this weekend. You have shown me a different way." He and his daughter rode away on his motorcycle.

I learned from this divine appointment that we are not to judge others; we are to love them with
Christ's love.

Bucket of Blessings

"And we know that all things work together for good to them who love God, to them who are called according to His purpose." Romans 8:28 (KJV)

I have been working in crisis pregnancy centers for 23 years. This ministry has taught me to walk entirely on faith. All of our funding to keep the doors open comes entirely from Christian people and churches who love God and life.

This miracle shows the creativity and humor of the God we serve. The rent was due for the center by Monday. It was Friday. I checked the bank statement and saw that we only had $200 left in our account. We needed $700 for the rent. God had taught me over the years that I am never to ask for the needs of the center but to thank Him for sending them.

My prayer that morning was a thank you Lord for sending the $500 needed for the rent. I also prayed that God would send the money creatively. You see I knew God could send the money in one check, but I like to see the creative side of God. I went to school and placed my cell phone on my desk. The phone rang. It was a man named Ray. Ray said he had a donation for the center and would my husband and I meet him at Hardees at 6:00 PM. He said I would need my husband help as the donation was heavy. I wondered if the donation was baby furniture. I called Ed and we met Ray at Hardees' at 6:00. He drove up in a handy man van. He called my husband over and they placed a five gallon bucket in my van. I thought, "What could possibly be in that bucket?" Ray took the lid off and the bucket was full of quarters. I smiled and asked God, "How much money is in there Lord?" He said He knew, but that I would have to count to find out the amount.

Ray told me he had been saving the quarters for a year. Ray said he got up and was having his morning devotion when God told him to get the bucket of quarters to the center today, it was needed. Guess how much money was in the bucket? God had sent $601 in a five gallon bucket to pay the rent for the center and He had done it creatively. I learned that my God has many ways to answer prayers. God is so unique and not limited in His ways.

Mount Diaper

"Bring ye all the tithes into the storehouse, that there may be meat in mine house, and prove me now herewith, saith the Lord of Hosts, if it will not open you the windows of heaven, and pour you out a blessing, that there shall not be room enough to receive it."
Malachi 3:10b (KJV)

Part of my job as a Director of a life ministry is to speak at churches and civic groups sharing about the crisis pregnancy ministry. On Sunday, I had spoken at a church in the morning and went to a baby shower at a different church that afternoon. I drove my daughter's compact car that Sunday and God blessed us at the baby shower with lots of baby items. It filled the car and I praised God for blessing these little ones with needed baby items. Just as I was about to get into my car, a little old lady came up to me and gave me $30 cash and told me to buy diapers for the babies. I thanked her and put the money in my purse. I remembered that there was a drug store that was changing companies and I would check the next day to see if they had some diapers for the ministry. I started the engine and God spoke to me. He said, "We are going to get the diapers today." I was not sure if I knew where the drug store was. I thought the manager would think I was crazy walking in and asking for diapers. God reminded me that you have not because you ask not. I walked into the store and found the manager.

I asked him for diapers for the babies at the center. I showed him the $30 and asked him to give me as many diapers as the money would buy. This tall man started crying, and I thought I must have hurt his feelings. You see this manager was a Christian, he had been in the storage room where there were rows of diapers that were not his brand. He had just prayed, "Lord, what am I going to do with all these diapers?" He told me to stand there and he would get me some diapers. He came out with a big case of diapers. He smiled, and I tried to give him the money. He said, "Lady I am not finished yet." I stood there and he said he would be right back. The manager went back and forth 12 times bringing cases of diapers. I stood and I knew that my God had done a miracle just like the fishes and loaves.

I counted the diapers and found that there were 3300 diapers. I asked him, "How much do I owe you for the diapers, Sir?" He smiled and said, "That will be $30 cash." I said, "Is there any tax?" He shook his head no and walked away singing. I stood there in amazement of an awesome God who cared that babies have dry behinds. I looked at the mountain of diapers and praised God. People walking by just stared at me. What was a 50 year old woman going to do with all those diapers? How was I going to get all these diapers to the center? My little car was already full. I simply said, "God, are you still here?" He replied, "Helen I said I would never leave you or forsake you. I have someone coming to get the diapers. Just stand here, she will be here in a few minutes." In about ten minutes, a teacher friend of mine walked in and walked over to me. She told me she had been asleep on the couch and God woke her up and told her to come to me. I had not seen her in a year. She looked at me and then she looked at the mountain of diapers and said, "What is that?" I told her-my question first. What was she driving? She told me she had her van. I said that was good because God had sent her to help take this mountain of diapers to the center. She did and many precious babies were blessed because of an awesome and mighty God who meets every need in our lives.

I learned that when God asks you to do something, He has a plan and a blessing. God had a divine appointment for the manager and I to meet that day. Two prayers were answered and many babies were blessed.

Special Delivery

"But my God shall supply all your needs according to his riches in glory by Christ Jesus." Philippians 4:19 (KJV)

I speak in many churches each month about the crisis pregnancy ministry. Six months earlier I had spoken at a church where the local postmaster attended. We were in need of diapers and formula for the centers and I had prayed that God would send these items. I got a call from the local postmaster that they had samples of diapers and formula left over at the post office. He said that they had several boxes of samples and they needed to get rid of them. He asked if we could use them at the center. I shouted, "YES!" I asked my husband to go by and pick them up the next day. He took the big truck thinking that would haul the diapers and formula. When he got to the post office, there were thousands of individually wrapped diapers and cases of formula. The diapers and formula filled the bed of the truck and even the cab. Praise God! Isn't it wonderful that God has Christians in the post office? Before we pray, God already has our needs on the way. God uses all ways to bless His children.

From Death to Life

"For His anger endureth but a moment; in His favour is life: weeping may endure for a night, but joy cometh in the morning." Psalm 30:5 (KJV)

My husband and I have been involved in starting crisis pregnancy centers in several counties in North Carolina. Ed is a pastor and we felt the call to come to Fayetteville, North Carolina. We started the Agape Pregnancy Support Services in a house on Cedar Creek Road. After we had been there for two years something happened to change our location. Fayetteville was the home of an abortion clinic that had been there for twenty-seven years. Many thousands of babies died in that clinic. Many Christians in the community would drive by the clinic and pray that the doors would close. God did answer their prayers and the doors of the clinic closed. The building was abandoned and the homeless would sneak into the building at night. It was a horrible place. One night I was restless so I decided to read. My daughter had given me a book called The Dream Giver by Dr. Bruce Wilkerson. In the book the author talks about getting out of our comfort zone and walking by faith. The next morning God asked me to get out of my comfort zone and go purchase the old abortion building. I told God I didn't want that building, I asked if He didn't have a new building we could have. I said, "Lord this is a place of death." God said, "I have a special plan for this place. I am going to take back what Satan has used for evil and redeem it. I will bring life from this place and it will bring glory and honor to me." I called the number on the building and asked the price. The price was $120,000. I reminded God that I was a kindergarten teacher and I had only a few dollars until payday. I knew that God would have to provide the money. God promised if we walked by faith, He would provide the money. Ed and I went to the old building, it was a horrible mess. It was trashed with drug needles, beer, wine and liquor bottles, rags, condoms, human feces where the homeless had stayed.

The windows were boarded up and it was very dark. We walked into the building carrying flashlights. You could feel the demonic powers in the place. We walked through the building shinning the light into each room. Each room had a plan and God revealed what it would be used for. At the back of building, there were two procedure rooms with Formica walls and drainage in the floor. One procedure room had equipment left with blood on it and blood on the Formica walls. I stood at the door feeling as if I was going to throw up. God said, "You have to go into the room. You must feel what I feel." As I walked into the room, I could feel the pain and the sorrow." I heard the babies crying because they didn't get to live the life that God had planned for them. They were also crying because they missed their Moms. I heard the Moms crying because they had killed their children. The third voice I heard in that room was my Lord and Savior weeping for all that was lost. My answer was "Yes". He reminded me it would be hard and the cost would be great. The answer was still, "Yes!" One month later my Mom died. God revealed that these two procedure rooms would be an ultra-sound room and the other a Chapel. The Chapel would be a place for women to come and find the forgiveness for their abortions. It would be a place to come out of the darkness into the light of Jesus. A man in our church did purchase the building and we make payments each month. We started working on the building. We anointed every room in the building. We prayed, painted, and cleaned all for the glory of Jesus.

The first room to get the boards off the windows was the Chapel. As the boards came down, the light of Jesus flooded the Chapel and the building. You could feel that Jesus had reclaimed what the enemy had for a season. I told my husband, "Look honey, there goes the Devil with his packed bags and he will not be coming back to this place."

The Agape Pregnancy Support Services is on the tough side of town. We have prostitutes, drug addicts, pimps and the homeless walking the streets in front of the building. I had a dear Christian lady to ask me if I knew what side of town the center was in. I smiled and said, "Yes, I do. I am exactly where Jesus would be." We know that God has placed us at this place. We are able to minister to the people of the streets and our clients. I see God taking people from death to life eternally just as He did with this old abortion clinic. God is the author of Life both physical and eternal.

Yvonne

"What shall we then say to these things? If God be for us, who can be against us?" Romans 8:31 (KJV)

We opened the doors to the new center called the Agape Pregnancy Support Services. It was awesome to see that the Lord had taken an old abortion clinic and turned it into a crisis pregnancy center. Many babies had died in this place, now it was a place of life for the babies as well as the Moms. At the Open House, we had a woman to walk in and asked for a tour of the building. She said she wanted to see what it looked like now. She had been one of the prostitutes who had used the building to abort three of her children. After the abortion clinic had closed, she had used the abandoned building as a party and drug place. As she walked through the building, she said she felt life and light. She accepted Jesus and has since cleaned up her life.

She now attends a local church. Her desire is to help others who walk on the streets to find the peace, life and light of Jesus Christ. It wasn't long after the meeting that our windows were broken out in the back of the building. When the police came, he asked me who I had been sharing Jesus with. I told him everyone that comes into the building. I shared about the prostitute, he told me that was the reason the windows were broken. You made the pimp mad. I thought if God allows me to stay at this center, I pray many more prostitutes and even the pimps will come to know Jesus as their Savior.

Heidi

"So teach us to number our days, that we may apply our hearts unto wisdom." Psalm 90:12 (KJV)

Ed and I had 2 biological children and 2 foster children when we found that we were expecting a baby in October. We were so excited! I carried this little one for 39 weeks when all of a sudden the doctor gave us the bad news that the health of our little baby was in danger. He sent me to Chapel Hill where an ultrasound and lots of tests were done. They determined that our precious little baby girl had lots of genetic defects. The doctors wanted to know if we wanted an abortion. The answer to that was "NO!" God is the author of life and death not man. I delivered at Chapel Hill which is known for giving care to babies that are in distress. They had to do a C-section on me since natural birth might cause more stress on my little one. From the time, I entered the hospital until the time I went home, there was a nurse who waited on me. She was in the delivery room and on the maternity hall. Her name was Heidi. I loved that name and asked her if I could name my little girl Heidi. She smiled and said that she was honored. Heidi Michelle Rogers came into the world weighing only 4 pounds. She was beautiful on the outside but on the inside she had lots of health problems. Organs were not in the right place and lungs were not developed. I was in a daze during that time. I had been in the hospital for five days as our little Heidi struggled in intensive care. The doctors told me that I would be going home the next day but my little Heidi would not be going. I told Ed to go home and rest, he had been with me the entire time and he as so tired. My prayer that last night in the hospital was, "Dear God, I can't go home without my precious Heidi. Please make her well enough to go home with me tomorrow or please come and take her to her heavenly home with you. She is so sick." God told me to go to the intensive are unit and to hold Heidi one last time that He was coming to get her. I hurt as I struggled to get to the third floor. I picked her up which was hard as she was hooked up to so many machines. I held her and rocked her and shared with her how much I loved her. I told her that she was going to heaven with Jesus and she smiled. I promised that one day we all would be in heaven together. I hugged and kissed her as she was passed to the nurse to hook back up to all the machines.

My heart was breaking. I returned to my room, and laid down on the bed. Suddenly a light filled the room. I heard Jesus say, "Heidi is with me now. She will never suffer again." Ten minutes later two doctors came into my room and said, "Mrs. Rogers, your little one has died." I shared with them that I already knew that God had revealed it to me. They looked surprised.

I went home the next morning. We had a little funeral and we sang Jesus Loves Me. Heidi was so beautiful in her white dress. Life went on as I had four children to take care of and a teaching job to get back to. I would teach all day, take care of my children and husband, and when everyone was in bed, I would sit in the rocking chair and rock a teddy bear that had been given to Heidi at the hospital and cry.

I kept asking God, "Why did Heidi have to be sick and have to leave us so soon?" He would comfort me and I could feel God's Daddy arms around me. One night as I rocked, I heard God say, "I have a special plan for Heidi's life and death. Yes it was short, yet her life will account for much. I am calling you into a ministry where women have lost babies to death not because it was my plan but by abortion. You will be able to feel their pain and walk with them through the hurt." Not long after that conversation God called me into crisis pregnancy ministries. Every time I share with a pregnant Mom and she chooses life, I can hear my little Heidi say, "Go, Mommy, tell them that she is carrying a precious baby." Since that time,

I have been godmother to around 10,000 babies in all shapes, sizes and colors.

God did have an awesome plan for Heidi's life and for me. Remember the nurse named Heidi that I named my little girl after. I went back to the hospital to thank her. Guess what? Therewas no nurse named Heidi who worked at that hospital. I believe that God sent me a beautiful angel to minister to me during this difficult time in my life. God has since blessed me with a beautiful granddaughter named Heidi Elizabeth. Now I have two Heidis, one who waits for me in heaven and one to love and play with here on earth. God can and does use the valleys in our lives to bring honor and glory to HIM!

Heart's Desire

"Delight thyself also in the Lord and He shall give thee the desires of thine heart." Psalm 37:4
(KJV)

One of the first crisis pregnancy centers we helped start was in Sanford, North Carolina. I was a volunteer in an established center in Rocky Mount and God sent us to Pittsboro. I looked for a center to volunteer in and God laid it on our hearts to start a center in Sanford. God walked us through the entire process and the center was up and ready in six months. I was so excited! I waited three weeks and no one came to the center. I asked God to please encourage me and let me know if this is what He had told me to do.

The phone rang and a young woman asked if we did abortions. I told her we did not do abortions nor do we refer for abortions. I did ask her if I could talk to her. We talked and I asked her," How did you find our number? You see we were not in anyone's phone book yet." She shared that she was crying and God gave her our number. I asked her what she thought she was going to have. Her reply was a little girl and she would have named her Destiny. We talked about God's plan for her and Destiny. She shared that she was a college student and lived about 40 miles from Sanford. Her parents did not know about the baby and the boyfriend wanted nothing to do with the baby. We talked some more and I referred her to a local crisis pregnancy center near her. That was the last time I heard from her. I did asked God to please let me see this Destiny. I know I cannot see all the babies that we help, but I desired to see this Destiny. Life went on and the Center got very busy. Often I would think of Destiny and her mother and lift up a prayer. Three years later, God moved us to a small community near the coast of North Carolina. God placed me in a hard place. Most of the children from this area were at risk with the basic needs of love, discipline, and Jesus was missing in their lives. I met prejudice from the other side. I was the token white woman on the staff. I fell in love with these needy kids and God blessed my time there. During the time we were there, Ed accepted a new church as pastor some fifty miles away from this area and I commuted back and forth. I prayed that God would release me from this place so I could find a school closer to our new home. God's answer was "NO, NOT YET!" He said that He had a divine appointment for me if I stayed another year. On the first day of school, I had a class of 28 students and the office called and said I had another student on the way to my room. I always greeted my students by bending down and introducing myself before I greeted the parents. In walked this beautiful petite black girl with the biggest smile and deep dimples. I bent over and said, "Hi! My name is Mrs. Rogers and I will be your new kindergarten teacher this year." She looked up at me with those beautiful brown eyes and said, "My name is Destiny!" My heart did flip flops and I knew that this was my Destiny. I looked up hoping to find her mother but found her grandmother instead. I asked where her mother was. The grandmother told me how her only daughter died in a car accident two years before and that Destiny was her only Grandchild. We hugged and cried together as I shared the story of the phone conversation of five years ago. Needless to say Destiny was the teacher's pet that year. God does give us our heart's desires if we will only listen and obey.

Love is Color-Blind

"My little children, let us not love in word, neither in tongue; but in deed and in truth" 1 John 3:18 (KJV)

Karen and Stephen fell in love in high school and she got pregnant at 16. Their families were not happy because number one they were young and she was pregnant. The other reason because it was interracial union. Both families were determined that Karen should have an abortion. Since Karen would not abort the baby, the parents wanted nothing to do with the teenagers. Karen came to the center feeling alone and ashamed. I started meeting with both of them and found that their love for each other was real. I encouraged them to continue to go to school. They both got part time jobs. Karen and Stephen were both Christians. Karen gave birth to a beautiful baby boy named Stephen. The healing of the families started when they held there precious grandchild. Stephen and Karen got married and Stephen joined the air force. Stephen and Karen would come and let me see baby Stephen. Stephen moved his family to Germany and I didn't see them for a long while. One day I got a surprise visit from Karen's Mom. She had made homemade blankets for the babies at the center. She thanked us for caring and loving her daughter when she did not. She said, "I can not imagine my world without my precious grandson." God is good! Our scripture says it, love is the key to all that is right and good.

God Speaks Chinese

"The Lord openeth the eyes of the blind: the Lord raiseth them that are bowed down: the Lord loveth the righteous." Psalm 146:8 (KJV)

We had just opened the doors of the new crisis pregnancy center in Sanford. I prayed to God that His name would be honored and glorified. One day I was surprised to have a Chinese woman walk into the center. She had the word, "Abortion" written on the piece of paper in her hands. I tried to tell her that we did not perform abortions. She could not speak English and I could not speak Chinese. I prayed to God and asked Him what to do. God told me to write down the next day's date and a time on the piece of paper. She took the paper and left thinking she was coming the next day for an abortion. When she walked out of the center, I fell to my knees and prayed that God would send me a Chinese Christian before the appointment of the next day. The small town of Sanford only had a few Chinese in it and they worked at the local restaurant. The young woman who had come in was a relative of these families. As I prayed, the phone rang and I answered the phone. There was a woman on the phone that I did not know. She told me that God had told her to call this number. She asked me if she could help. I told her that I had been praying for a Chinese Christian to talk to a young lady who wanted an abortion. She was quiet for a minute and then she shared that she was the Pastor at a Chinese Church in the adjacent county. I asked her if she would talk to this young lady the next morning by phone and tell her that we did not do abortions. I asked her to share with the young lady the message of life for her and her baby. She said she would do better than that. She told me she would meet me the next morning at the Center. I thanked her and praised God for always being an on-time God.

The next morning I went early to the center so I could pray for the appointment. Guess what, when I got to the center the young Chinese woman was there with her boyfriend. The Chinese pastor arrived and took the young couple into the counseling room. I listened as the Pastor shared with this couple the message of Life for her child and the eternal message for the young man and woman. I did not understand the words, but I felt the Holy Spirit working and moving in that room. It was a beautiful morning. The young couple agreed to come to her church to hear more about this Jesus. As far as I know, she did not abort the baby. They married and the baby lived. I prayed that the young couple accepted Jesus. I will not know that answer until I get to Heaven. I discovered that day that nothing is impossible for my Heavenly Father. If you are in need, your Heavenly Father has heard your prayer and the answer is on the way.

One Baby's Worth

"For it is God which worketh in you both to will and to do of His good pleasure." Philippians 2:13 (KJV)

Our work continues at the center as God blesses us with women who are in need of His love and guidance. One rainy cold night a young woman named Jane stood at the door of the center crying. She held in her hand "Blood Money" that her boyfriend had given her to abort the child she was carrying. We invited her in and dried her off. Jane and I talked about the life she was carrying in her womb. I told her that even though this earthly father did not want his son, I knew a Heavenly Father who would take care of her and the baby. She accepted Jesus that night as her Lord and Savior. We continued to meet during the pregnancy as we prayed and talked about God's love. She took parenting classes, read her Bible, and started attending a local Church. As her figure grew, so did her love for her baby and her Lord. Jane called me early one Easter morning and said, "Come quick, Miss Helen, my baby is coming." I rushed to the hospital but baby Andrew was already born. I walked in Jane's room; she picked up baby Andrew and placed him in my arms. She looked at Andrew and said, "Andrew, this is Miss Helen, I would have killed you if God had not placed her in my life to tell me that you are a precious gift from God. I found life for you son and found eternal life in Jesus." As I held baby Andrew I thought to myself, "Is this child worth all the time and energy to save him?:" The answer was "YES!". I thought about all the times we wait at the center for the clients, the speaking at churches and all the prayers. If there had been only one baby in all these years who needed saving from an abortion, Andrew was worth it.

Jane continued to come to the center for emotional support, encouragement and love. God allowed her to go back to school part time and work part time and raise her child. Many times she would ask me if God had a Christian man for her to marry. I assured her that He did. She kept coming to the center. One day she shared that she had met a young man at church and they were dating. Their relationship grew into love and I was invited to the October wedding. I signed in at the register, baby Andrew was sitting in his seat smiling at all who came in. It was as if he knew that he was getting an earthly Daddy. Jane walked down the aisle with Andrew cooing. You see Sam not only married Jane, he accepted Andrew as his son. Today this precious family is serving the Savior as a pastor's family. If we are faithful to follow God, even when it looks dark, God always blesses in more ways than we can count.

God's Box

"Cast thy bread upon the waters: for thou shalt find it after many days."
Ecclesiastes 11:1 (KJV)

Pregnancy ministries are always in need of maternity clothes. I prayed and asked God to please send us a box of maternity clothes. When I got home from the center that night, there was a message from a man I did not know. I called and he shared with me that his Mom had a maternity shop before she died. He wanted to know if we could use the maternity clothes at the pregnancy center. We made an appointment to pick up the clothes at the end of the week. Much to our surprise, we picked up 4400 pieces of brand new maternity clothes with the tags still on them. He gave us the entire inventory of the shop. We shared some of these clothes with other ministries in the area and used the rest for the Moms at the center. I learned that day that the size of my box and the size of God's box are quite different. I also have learned to ask God for whatever box He wants to send. What a big God we serve! Don't ever limit God, let God be God!

Money from Heaven

"What shall we say to these things? If God be for us, who can be against us" Romans 8:31 (KJV)

Money was scare and payday was two weeks away. I wanted to give one of our clients a wedding gift. She had chosen life for her child by parenting. She and her boyfriend had decided to get married. We were having the wedding at the center. I prayed and asked God to send me $20.00. I was walking across the parking lot and there on the ground was a $20.00 bill. I picked it up and looked around to see if anyone had dropped it. There was no one around. I started raising my hands in praise. A car drove by and a man asked me if I was okay. I smiled and showed him the $20.00 bill that God sent. God had answered my prayer and rained money from heaven. God is the Provider and will supply all our needs according to His riches in glory. Thank you Jesus, you are a creative God.

Seven Abortions

"He will swallow up death in victory and the Lord God will wipe away tears from off all faces; and the rebuke of His people shall he take away from off all the earth: for the Lord hath spoken it." Isaiah 25:8 (KJV)

The Agape Pregnancy Support Services building used to be an abortion clinic for 27 years. God took the old abandoned building and turned it into a life ministry. Many times we have had women who have experienced abortions at this location to come back. Joyce was one of these women. She called and asked if she could have a tour of the building. I noticed that as I showed her the rooms she began to cry. Finally I took her to the old procedure room that is now a Chapel. She sobbed and that is when I asked her, "Joyce, you have been here before, haven't you?" She looked at me and said, " I have had five abortions in this room. You see I was the homecoming queen, student body president, when I was in high school. Nobody knew that I was sexually active and that I was aborting my children. I hid it from my family and friends.

My last abortion was the worst one. The doctor gave me a medicine to deliver a dead baby. I returned at 4:45 with cramps. The doctor was bloody and he had been drinking. He was angry with me for being there so late. He put me on the table. I screamed, "I don't want an abortion!" The doctor

God Loves You Better Than Mac And Cheese 33

said you paid for it and you will get it. He finished the abortion and gave me a cup of kool-aid and a cookie and sent me out the door.

Later on, I moved to Colorado where I had two more abortions. Jesus came into my life and I realized that I had murdered seven of my children. I am now working in a life ministry in Colorado. I have asked God to forgive me and I believe that coming back to this place is part of my healing." Joyce added her children's names to the Memorial Wall. She left and you could see the healing had begun.

I have never met a woman who was glad she aborted her baby. I only see the pain and sorrow of that choice. There are many women who have aborted children and they are called "the walking wounded." If you have had an abortion, please get help with a counselor or visit your local pregnancy center.

Seeing with God's eyes

"I call heaven and earth to record this day against you, that I have set you life and death, blessings and cursing: therefore choose life, that both thou and thy seed may live." Deuteronomy 30:19 (KJV)

The crisis pregnancy ministry allows us to meet with women from all ethnic and social backgrounds. Agnes walked into the center looking for an abortion. She had four children already. Agnes only had one living with her because she had given away three of her children to get more drugs. The one she had at home was not getting cared for. Now she was pregnant again. She had no idea of the name of the father of the baby she was carrying. As we talked, I saw all the heartache of sin's hold in her life. I asked God to give me spiritual eyes so I could see what He saw in Agnes. God showed me a beautiful woman of God caring for all of her children and serving Him. I saw royalty, a princess of the Most High God. I got excited and asked if I could tell her what God saw in her. She covered her face and said, "I am afraid of what God sees in me. " I told her that God loved her and He had wonderful plans for her life. We talked of a Savior who left Heaven's glory to take our sins upon Himself and then died on a cross for those sins-all of them. God chose to die for her because of His great love for her. She accepted Jesus that night. She started going to church, cleaned up her life of drugs and alcohol. She found all her children and they became a family that served Jesus. She became a godly Mother and woman. She met a man at church and later married him. The entire family is serving God. God made us special. We are made in His image. Let's look the people we meet with the eyes of God. Have you asked God what He sees in you? Ask and He will WOW you!

The Greatest Gift

"And the Lord, He it is that doth go before thee; he will be with thee, he will not fail thee, neither forsake thee, fear not, neither be dismayed." Deuteronomy 31:8 (KJV)

Many times I am called to the local hospitals to deliver layettes to needy Moms and babies. One evening I got a call from Miss Debbie, the social worker at the hospital. There was a 14 year old girl who had just delivered a baby girl. Her parents had thrown her out and her 21 year old boyfriend had deserted her and she was all alone. I made a basket of baby items to take to her because she had nothing for the baby. I knocked on her door, and heard a quiet come in. I found a very young 14 year old crying with a beautiful baby girl in her arms. I showed her the basket and she wanted to know where it came from. I told her " Jesus sent you this. He loves you and your precious little girl. He is going to care for you both." Her reply was, "I have heard about this Jesus all my life, usually in profanity. Do you know Jesus?" I told her that Jesus was my Lord and Savior. I shared with her the plan of salvation and she accepted Jesus as her Savior. As I turned to leave, I said, "You have given your baby the greatest gift of all and that is the gift of a mother who loves Jesus." I thought to myself as I left that room, she is a 14 year old girl with an infant baby, her parents and her boyfriend has abandoned her, but she now has everything. She has Jesus.

The young girl and her baby were both placed in foster care together. I think of her often and I pray that she has seen God's plan and provision for her life.

Precious Memories

"Lo, children are an heritage of the Lord: and the fruit of the womb is his reward."
Psalm 127:3 (KJV)

I have two precious granddaughters and I have one precious grandson on earth. Five years ago, God gave us a grandson for a little while. Here is the letter I read at his funeral. There maybe someone that is reading this that is hurting from the loss of a child. Remember Jesus is our Hope and our only Hope.

Dear Adam,

We just want you to know we love you and we already miss you. You came into our lives about 8 months ago when your Mom told us we were going to have a new grandchild. We were so excited. You see, Kassi, your little sister asked Santa for a baby. That did not work, so she decided to ask God for a baby sister. In January we found out that God had answered Kassi's prayers. We started guessing if you were a boy or girl.

We were so excited! Kassi and Heidi finally decided that a baby brother was okay. Marsha started going for appointments keeping us updated on the progress of this new addition to our family. We prayed that your life would honor God

Then one day in April, we got the terrible news, that you our precious grandson had lots of health problems and the doctors gave you zero percent chance of living. I remember weeping and praying for you. You see the doctors thought you would die in the womb. But Adam, we know the Heavenly Father and we prayed for your healing. And God did heal you sweetheart so you could stay with us for a little while. Kassi and Heidi's prayers consisted simply of "God take care of baby Adam." Many people were praying for you.

I want you to know, Adam, that your Mom and Dad fought to give you life. The doctors wanted to abort you but your Mama and Daddy said that God is the author of life and death. They trusted God with His plan for you. They did all that was humanly possible for you. Adam, we prayed for your healing and God did heal you. Even now you are in the arms of Jesus; you are whole and in no pain.

Adam, you were perfect to us. You were so cute with tiny hands, reddish blond hair, Kelvin's toes, and that cute little smile. Mama and Daddy named you Joshua Adam which means Saved by the Lord and made in the image of God. You fought so hard to stay with us. I watched your little heart rate go up as your Daddy and Mama held you and talked to you. We all watched as your heart rate would go down again and then your sisters would sing "Jesus Loves Me" to you and the rate would become steady again.

Adam, many people will not understand how we could love you so deeply since in their eyes you only lived five hours. In our hearts, you lived eight months of this Earth, and now you will be a part of our life forever. Adam you taught us about life and love. Little One, all babies should have what you had, a safe place to grow inside your Mom, a loving family, and a big God. You have made this family stronger in love and helped us to re-dedicate our lives fighting for other babies in the womb. Thanks Adam, we love you!

I remember asking God one day, "Why did my little Adam die?" God said, "I have a plan for Adam's life just as I do for all my people." Whether you live one minute, five hours or 100 years, it should be all for God's Glory. Because we love Jesus, Adam, we simply will say we will see you soon.

Forever in our Hearts,

Love, your family

PS Five years later God blessed us with a grandson named Cole. Now I have a grandson in heaven and one to play with down here. God is so good!

Heavenly Haircut

"In everything give thanks: for this is the will of God in Christ Jesus concerning you." 1 Thessalonians 5:18 (KJV)

The Crisis Pregnancy Ministries gets very busy and sometimes I don't get to take a minute even for a haircut. My hair was in need of trimming to cut the dead ends off. I was working all day as a kindergarten teacher and then working in the life ministries until 9:00 each night. There was no time to go and get a haircut. I prayed a simple prayer, "Lord, please send someone to the center to cut my hair."

The next week, I was working at the center when a lady came in with a case in her hand. I asked if I could help her. She said that God had told her to come and give me a haircut. She cut it right there in the reception room of the center. I asked her how much I owed her. She said, "No charge!" smiled and walked out of the center. I did not know her and I have never seen her since. Do you think God has angel beauticians? We have not because we ask not!

The Nightmare

"….for I am not come to call the righteous, but sinners to repentance."
Matthew 9:13 (KJV)

I speak at many churches and groups about the pregnancy ministries. In all these years, I have never met a woman who was glad she had an abortion.

Not so long ago, I met an 81 year old woman who had nine children, lots of grandchildren and great-grandchildren. Her life was full of family but she had a dark secret she had never shared. When she was sixteen, she got pregnant out of wedlock. Her family obtained a secret abortion for her so that no one would know. She knew and it was etched in her heart forever. She told of the nights she cried for the child she had killed. Her nights were filled with nightmares of the abortion and the cries of her child.

She had many more children, but there was still a missing piece of her heart. In this pregnancy ministry we call the women who have had abortions "the walking wounded." The woman has finally accepted the forgiveness from God and has forgiven herself. God is the only one who can heal the broken hearts of the women who have had abortions. Once the truth comes to the light, the devil has no more hold over you.

Is there something in your life you have hidden and you are in need of healing? Give it to Jesus!!

Hope

"But God, who is rich in mercy, for his great love wherewith he loved us, Even when we were dead in sins, hath quickened us together with Christ, (by grace ye are saved;)" Ephesians 2:4-5 (KJV)

One of the pregnancy centers that we work with is not on the sunny side of town. It is in the middle of pimps, prostitutes, and drug addicts. We not only witness to the clients who come to our door, we go out to the streets and witness. One of these ladies-of-the-evening was named Priscilla. She would come to us for food and clothes. We would feed her and find warm clothes for her. One night she came in and she was crying. It was very cold outside. She asked if she could lay down on one of the couches to rest because she had not been able to sleep. You see she had been sleeping under the bridge and the men under the bridge would take turns raping her. She slept a while and then, I talked to her. She told me she was six months pregnant. She was carrying twins, but because of the rapes she had lost one of her babies.

I said, "Priscilla, don't you think it is time to ask Jesus into your life?" You have been running from Him for a long time. "She started crying and said she did want Christ in her life. I usually take the hands of the person I am praying for. She took my hands and put them on her head. She said, "I want Jesus all over me- from the top of my head to the bottom of my feet."

She prayed the sinner's prayer and you could see the difference. She left that night, and I did not see her for two months.

I work at another center in an adjacent county. I was there on a Tuesday night and who should come in but Priscilla. She looked well; she was clean, healthy and was smiling. We hugged each other and I asked her where she had been. She had checked herself into a Christian Woman's Ministry that housed women in need. I gave her a layette for her baby and a car seat. I asked Priscilla what she was going to name her baby. She said, "My baby girl's name is Hope. Jesus gave me baby Hope and He gave me hope for my life." When the baby was born, she could not take care of her baby. She found a local pastor and wife and they took baby Hope. Priscilla made a good decision for herself and for baby Hope. God has a good plan for Priscilla and baby Hope. If you have been running from Jesus, it is time to stop running away but run to Jesus. He is your only HOPE!

Amy's Miracle

"For it is God which worketh in you both and to do of his good pleasure."
Philippians 2:13 (KJV)

We get many requests from many social agencies asking if we can help needy families. One day we received a call from a Hospice nurse. She had a tiny patient who weighed a little over two pounds. Amy was her name and she had been born with her brain on the outside of her head and with other complications. The Hospice nurse wanted to know if we had a certain formula used for preemies that is very expensive. She was also looking for preemie diapers. I told her that we did not have either of these items at present but I knew that God would provide for this precious child. I told her to come to the center at 7:00 that night and God would have the items needed for Amy.

God is always an on time God. At 6:55, a van pulled up in our yard with 10 cases of the needed formula and 12 cases of preemie diapers. We just took the items and moved them to the Hospice nurse's car. Amy lived long enough to use the items that God sent. God always provides for His little ones and for you. His love is so great that He even cares that a tiny person has the simple things like diapers and formula. God knows your need. He will answer your prayers on time-His time.

The Not So Good Abraham

"I say unto you, that likewise joy shall be in heaven over one sinner that repenteth, more than over ninety-nine just persons, which need no repentence." Luke 15:7 (KJV)

The Agape Pregnancy Support Services is on a tough side of Fayetteville. We have pimps, prostitutes, drug addicts, and alcoholics walking the streets in front of the center. We try to reach out to these lost people by sharing the Word and food.

One day a man walked in with a young woman and wanted to know if she could get a pregnancy test. He was her pimp and if she was pregnant, he was going to make her abort the child. I started to take the young woman to the counseling room but God stopped me. He said, "Stay here and talk to the pimp." I argued with God for a minute and finally agreed to talk to him. I introduced myself and found out his name was Abraham. I asked God if He would sit in Abraham's lap until we finished our conversation. I smiled as I saw Jesus sit in his lap. I asked him who prayed for him. He said that his grandmother did. I told him that I knew what he did for a profession. He started to get up but could not get out of the chair. I told him that Jesus was sitting in his lap until we finished. I asked him if he knew the mighty story of Abraham from the Bible. He wept as he told me the story of his life. Drugs, sex, and greed had ruled him all his life.

He listened as I shared the Good News of God's Grace and Forgiveness. I told him of ultimate sacrifice on the cross for all sins and that the debt was paid in full. We had prayer and I knew that the seeds of truth were planted that day. We finished and then he looked at me and asked if he could get up now. I said, "Yes!" He almost ran out of the building saying, "That was the craziest thing that ever happened to me. Imagine Jesus sitting in my lap and wanting to live in my life." He walked away hopefully not the same way he had come in. I still pray for Abraham. I will tell you that I have not seen him on the streets since his encounter with Jesus.

Diapers from Heaven

"For the kingdom of God is not in word but in power." 1 Corinthians 4:20 (KJV)

One night at the pregnancy ministry a young Muslim woman came in and asked for a pack of size four diapers. I sat down across from her to counsel with her. She told me she did not want to hear anything about that Jesus stuff. She said "I am Muslim and I just came here for diapers." I asked her why she didn't go to a Muslim pregnancy center instead of a Christian one. She told me that there are not any Muslim pregnancy centers. I told her that we didn't have any size four diapers but let's talk.

I started the conversation by asking her about her religious beliefs. I asked her what she had to do to go to heaven. She gave me a long list of rules and sacrifices and even if she followed them all, she wasn't sure of Heaven. I told her about the steps to Jesus 1. By believing Jesus died on the cross for your sins 2. Knowing that you are a sinner who needs a Savior. 3. Asking Jesus to come into your heart and life. I told her that I was absolutely sure that I was going to Heaven because of my relationship with Jesus. She listened. Finally she said, "If there is a real Jesus then there will be a pack of size four diapers for me tonight." She was challenging my God. I reminded her that there were not any four diapers but that I would go and pray for some. I went to the backroom and looked everywhere hoping that there was a size four pack hiding somewhere.

I prayed "God show her who you are by providing a pack of size four diapers. God please don't send size three diapers or size five diapers, just fours." God whispered in my ear that He had saved me a pack of size four diapers at the back of a file cabinet that was in the storage room. I rushed over to the file cabinet and there were the size four diapers. I praised God and ran back to the counseling room. I held up the size four diapers and said, "See there is a real Jesus and He just provided you with diapers for your baby." I wish you could have seen her face. She turned to leave and said, "I would like to know more about this Jesus." God is a creative God. God sent manna from Heaven, why not diapers?

Sue's Story

"As the days wherein the Jews rested from their enemies, and the month which was turned unto them from sorrow to joy, and from mourning into a good day: that they should make them days of feasting and joy, and of sending portions one to another, and gifts to the poor." Esther 9:22a (KJV)

One of the clients who came to the pregnancy center was a young woman we will call Sue. Sue came in very downcast and sad. She needed a pregnancy test and the test came back positive. I asked her what she was going to do with the baby. She replied that she wanted to keep the baby but that the boyfriend wanted an abortion. She told me she had been a foster child and that her foster Dad had raped her when she was 15 years old. She got pregnant and the foster Dad took her for an abortion. She told of all the pain and regrets since that abortion.

Her life got tougher after that. She married the first young man who came along and showed her any attention. She had three children with this man. He was physically abusive to her and the children. He finally ended up in prison. She came to North Carolina looking for Christian families so she could place her children for adoption. Sue gave up custody of her children and that left her all alone and sad in a place she was not familiar with. A young policeman befriended her and she was now pregnant with his child.

I asked her if the father of the baby had come with her and she said he was in the waiting room.

I went out and asked the young man to come in. His reply was, "I'm not pregnant." I said, "Yes, you are." He sat down and I told him the results of the pregnancy test. I asked him what he wanted to do and he said he wanted an abortion. I looked at James and asked him, "What is an abortion son?" He hung his head and said it was the taking of a fetus. I asked James to look me straight in the eye and tell me what an abortion was. He said, "Abortion is the killing of a baby." I said, "Whose baby?" His reply was "Mine." He was 32 years old and I told him what he did with this baby would determine his manhood. He told me he knew abortion was wrong that he was a pastor's son. We talked and he agreed to let Sue put the baby up for adoption. They left and I continued to pray because I knew God was not finished yet. Sue called me half way through the pregnancy and said that James had agreed to let her keep the baby. Just before the baby was born Sue and James got saved, baptized, and married. James is studying to go into the ministry. Baby Jayden is alive, with godly parents who will teach him about a Savior who loves him.

Cole

"Delight thyself also in the Lord; and He shall give thee the desires of thine heart." Psalm 37:4 (KJV)

I have two beautiful granddaughters and one precious grandson in heaven. One day I went to the Lord in prayer and asked Him to please bless me with a grandson here on earth. I wanted one to play baseball with, catch frogs together and a little boy who would pee in my face when I changed his diaper. The Word says that God will give us the desires of our heart if you walk God's path. The prayer was answered and in two months Marsha, my daughter was pregnant. We were all so excited! This pregnancy would require lots of prayer as Marsha had lost 4 babies to death already. The pregnancy started and so did the tests and doctors' appointments. The time moved slowly along. In the eighth month, Marsha was given the news that there were problems with the baby. Many people were praying.

The day came and we went to the Delivery Room. The doctors and nurses were very concerned about the baby. They called for the intensive care unit for the baby believing that there was going to be problems. Marsha dilated two cm. and stopped. All were concerned for the baby and for Marsha as her blood pressure dropped too low. I started praying aloud and I could feel the flood of prayers from all the saints. God touched Marsha and the baby. Marsha stabilized and the dilation moved from 2 cm to 10 cm in 30 minutes. Our precious grandson, Cole came out whole and healthy. The intensive care unit was not needed. I had the blessing of cutting Cole's cord and I dedicated him to God's service.

I heard the nurse say, "Something happened when that Grandmother started praying." Heidi and Kassi, Cole's sisters sang Happy Birthday to him and Jesus Loves Me. Jesus is so wonderful and He will give us our heart's desires if we try to walk His path. Thank you Jesus!

The Eyes of a Child

"Blessed are the pure in heart, for they shall see God." Matthew 5:8 (KJV)

We have many volunteers who help us at the pregnancy ministry. Sometimes the volunteers bring their children with them. Nicole brings Joey, her three year old with her. He is full of life. Many times when he comes to the center, he sees me ministering to the prostitutes on the street outside of our building. They sometime will sit on the bench in our prayer garden. One day Joey came running into the center and said, "Miss Helen, Miss Helen, there is a girl sitting on our bench. She needs food and she needs Jesus." You see the girl he is talking about is a 55 year old prostitute. I told him I was getting some food together. He ran off to play in the playroom and I went outside to the woman. I gave her some food and tried to talk to her about Jesus again. She walked away again without Jesus.

A little later Joey came running into the counseling room and said, "Miss Helen, did you give the girl some food and tell her about Jesus?" I told him that I did and that we need to keep praying for the girl on the bench. He said, "Good, and that he would pray for her." Joey ran back to his world of play. You see Joey has the eyes of Christ. He did not see the woman's sins; he saw a girl hungry and one who needed Jesus. Why can't we be more like Joey with the people we meet in the world? God tells us not to judge but to see each person the way that God sees them.

Katie's Story

"For we walk by faith, not by sight:" 2 Corinthians 5:7 (KJV)

I met Katie at the crisis pregnancy center when she was four months pregnant. She was in a very abusive relationship with a young man who was trying to kill her. He had tried to run her car off the road, kidnapped her and locked her in his house and raped her several times. She was expecting a boy and she was afraid. My family and I hid her car at our house so he could not find her. Her family helped her during this time. Finally the day came when she had Greg; he was a beautiful baby boy. Katie continued to try to care for her baby and she was so proud of him. When Greg turned 18 months old, she found that her own father was molesting her son. She was so angry and completely cut all communication with her family. You see her father was sent to prison for rape and molesting children and Katie did not know it. The family had kept the secret from her.

Greg became my adopted grandchild and we continue to help Katie as she struggles to make ends meet. Her life became even more troubled and once again the unspeakable happened. She was raped and again she found she was pregnant. She talked of abortion and even went to the abortion clinic twice. Katie could not go through with the abortion. We walked through the pregnancy with her and she called as she went to the hospital. I went to the delivery room with her and prayed as little Sam came into the world. Once again, Katie fell in love with her little fellow. She said that she only saw love in him and not how he had started out.

Katie continues to look after her children. She is a good mom but has a hard time as she is on a fixed income with health problems. Some days she calls and cries saying "I can't do this anymore." We pray for one more day of strength. The children call me Grandma. I try to send some help each month. Katie is alone and scared of all the men she sees as she shops for groceries.

Christians do you know that there are Katies all around us? They are the ones who sit at the back of the church. They are the ones whose little boys are unruly and she needs help. She can not give to the church. She was sent by God for us to minister too. Will you look around your neighborhood or church and find the Katie you should be reaching out too?

A Friend's Story

"Bear ye one another's burdens, and so fulfill the law of Christ." Galatians 6:2 (KJV)

This is a story that a friend gave me to share so that others will choose life:

It was a cold day in October and according to my prediction I was already two months pregnant. I was facing the scariest time of my life and not knowing what to do or where to turn. Family would seem like the most logical place to turn but being raised in a religious family; this just wasn't the situation a good Christian girl would be in. The nights seemed longer and the days shorter as so many thoughts crossed my mind. Should I keep this baby, should I abort, should I run away, should I just end it all? Does a teenager in my shoes really have a choice? I later found myself confiding in the one family member that I thought I could trust and her way seemed like the easiest way out and that was to abort. "You can come spend a week with me as if nothing is wrong and when you return back home no one would ever know." She said, "You have your whole life ahead of you and you can't disappoint your family." Well she was right, what choice did I have, so I decided to abort something that had already became a part of me.

The week had come when it was time to go visit my aunt in what seemed to other family members like a routine visit but little did they know I would leave with two heartbeats and return with only one shattered one. The appointment was made and I can recall this being the longest night of my life. I laid there scared with doubts but thinking that I can't turn back now because the appointment had been made. The minutes seemed like hours as I laid there and watched the clock.

Soon it was about 7:00 and I could hear my aunt approaching the door. "Get up and get ready she said, we have about a 45 minute drive and your appointment is at 9:00." I laid there frozen when I felt something move inside of me. Could it really be a cry from deep within pleading for his or her life? I wondered as I arose from my bed and then there it was again.

I sat back down and said a soft prayer and I remember it as if it was yesterday. "God, I know I don't know you like I should but you know me. I need your understanding because I can't do this alone. Help me to make the right choice that would not cause me to regret or wonder what if. God, I don't know what lies ahead if I go through with this. Please give me a sign." Just then I felt a tug, as if it was the one last cry from the womb and then I knew.

When my aunt came to the door she found me sobbing on the side of the bed and she knew. She didn't pressure me or try to change the decision that was so obvious but only asked one last time, "Are you sure?" and my reply was "Yes!" She reminded me that it wouldn't be easy and all of the things that I would be giving up but now I had a choice.

Well as this story concludes, I chose life and now 21 years later that choice is an Honor Student in College preparing to graduate next year. I made a choice. He is gifted in vocals and plays the piano. I made a choice. He desires to give back to communities that are less fortunate. One day he wants to help young troubled boys get off the streets. I made a choice. He is now the proud brother of two little sisters that wouldn't be able to be who they are without their big brother. I made a choice and you can too. Life doesn't always deal us a perfect hand but God does. His hands are big enough to hold and handle anything. No matter how difficult it may seem, you have a choice. Don't just listen to your heart but also to that small, almost silent heart that beats in the background and I encourage you to Choose Life! Sincerely, A Very Proud Mother

The Double Sunflower

"Delight thyself also in the Lord and He shall give thee desires of your heart." Psalm 37:4 (KJV)

God says that if we serve Him and seek to follow His will for our lives that He will give us our heart's desires. I had always wanted a yellow Volkswagen since I was a teenager and that was a long time ago. Ed and I stopped by the VW dealership in Fayetteville. I asked the salesman if he had a used yellow Volkswagen bug. He said, "I will keep my eyes open but we don't get many used yellow VW's. I will call you if one comes in." I smiled, you see, absolutely nothing is impossible for my God.

Two days later I got a call from that young salesman. He said, "Mrs. Rogers, you won't believe this, but I have a special one of a kind VW 2002 model that came in today." This VW is unique in that only 1000 of these special VW's were made. It is called "Double Sunflower." A side note, Sunflowers are my favorites. The car has a yellow and black interior with special features. It even had a sunroof and was beautiful.

The salesman said that the other salesmen were trying to take it away from him. He told them that he had promised the car to me. I signed the papers and took it home. I had them put happy face decals on each door with scripture. One happy face says, "Rejoice in the Lord" and the other says "Smile God loves you." I also put on lots of life stickers. I have an awesome

God. He knew the gas prices were going to go sky high and I would need a car to carry me to work in these life ministries.

Everywhere I go people will stop and stare at this yellow God mobile. Some people really like it and we talk about Jesus at the red stoplights. Others do not like the car, and will hollow at me. I smile and point them to Jesus. I call my bug the God Mobile or Joy Bug. My license plate says, "JOYFUL ME!" God is my Joy.

Chloe

"Blessed are the pure in heart: for will they shall see God." Matthew 5:8 (KJV)

I retired from public school teaching after 34 years, then I taught in a Christian school for four years. One of my precious students was a beautiful little girl who had been adopted from China at the age of 22 months. Chloe is a twin, she had a sister in the other class. Chloe would always tell me that she had two Moms, one in China and one in America.

She said, "China Mom could not take care of us so she put us in an orphanage. Orphanage was not good, we got hurt there. America Mom, she got faith in God and got on airplane and come and get us." Chloe is a beautiful child with a heart of gold. She is so compassionate, caring and a peacemaker. I called her my China doll.

One day during devotion time. Trace asked me if the Bible had anything to say about heaven. I told him "yes" and read to the class from Revelation. I shared with them about the streets of gold and no pain in heaven. Brandon asked me if they had math in heaven. I told him if they did he would know all the answers. He liked that. I also told them that there was no electricity in heaven. They looked afraid until I told them that God was the light in heaven. There is no darkness. Zoe said, "I hear you get a new body when you go to heaven, Mrs. Rogers." I told her that was true and Mrs. Rogers was going to be skinny in heaven. They all smiled.

The next day Chloe was drawing a picture of me with red hair, blue eyes, and a big smiley face on my shirt. I was skinny. I said, "Chloe, you made Mrs. Rogers skinny." She smiled and said, "Mrs. Rogers, you are in heaven and you are skinny." God blesses us with the wisdom of children if we will only listen. There is always a smile if we look with children's eyes.

Thank you God for children.

Show Me My Baby

"Blessed are the pure in heart, for they shall see God." Matthew 5:8 (KJV)

Ultrasound machines can help expectant Moms see their precious babies in the womb. We had been praying for an ultrasound machine for the crisis pregnancy center. I went to speak at a church and a lady named Bobbi walked up to me. She was in her eighties. Bobbi said, "We need to talk." She said that God had told her to purchase an ultrasound machine for the center. She promised she would do the leg work to find the machine. Miss Bobbi contacted many companies and visited local doctor's offices to view the machines. There was urgency in her voice….."I need to get this done, I'm not a spring chicken anymore."

Miss Bobbi worked hard on this project. Our next meeting was a telephone conference with a representative from a company. We met and told the young man what we needed. He told her that he had the right one for the needs of the center. The salesman started to quote the price. Miss Bobbi said, "Wait a minute young man! I need to know if Jesus is in your life as your Lord and Savior." The salesman hesitated and answered "Yes." Miss Bobbi reminded him that the machine was for saving lives in this pregnancy ministry. He gave us a great price and now we are able to show Moms their precious babies in the wombs. You are never too old or too young to listen to God. Miss Bobbi did!

Kassi

"Train a child in the way he should go, and when he is old, he will not depart from it."
Proverbs 22:6 (KJV)

I include my precious granddaughters in the crisis pregnancy ministry. I want them to know that God created everyone. Sometimes they will go with me to fold baby clothes or make food bags. Kassi who was five years old at the time, was sitting at my desk. She was watching me help Moms and babies with material things and prayer. She looked at me and said, "Gega, who will help the babies when you die and go to heaven?" I looked at her and said, "Kassi, God will call someone else to be a crisis pregnancy director and help Moms and babies." She looked at me, "Gega I am going to be a crisis pregnancy center director when I grow up. Somebody has to tell the Moms about Jesus and about life for their babies."

I cannot leave money to my children and grandchildren but I desire to leave a legacy of Jesus. What are you leaving for the next generation?

What I Learned On The Farm

"For I know the thoughts that I think toward you, saith the Lord, thoughts of peace, and not of evil, to give you an unexpected end." Jeremiah 29:11 (KJV)

I was raised on a farm with parents who loved God and loved us. Dad taught me many lessons about God from the farm. One of my favorite ones is the plowing of the field. Daddy was plowing the field with a horse and a plow. He always plowed such nice neat rows. I was the oldest of five children and I thought I could plow a row too. I asked Dad if he would let me plow. He said yes with a smile. He handed me the reins and I started down the field making a row. I kept looking back to make sure I was doing okay. I completed the row and looked at my row. I had a very crooked row, it did not look like my Dad's rows.

I asked Dad why my row looked like a zigzag pattern and his rows were so straight. He said, "Do you see that old oak tree at the end of the row? Always keep your eyes on it as you plow. It is alright to occasionally look back to make sure the plow is working but don't stay back there. Keep your eyes straight ahead." I learned from Dad that day that God is the old oak tree we are to keep our eyes on as we walk through this life. It is okay to occasionally look back at the past, but don't make a hammock and stay there.

Learn from your past and share it with the ones who need to be encouraged. God's path is straight and full of excitement. Jeremiah 29:11 says "For I know the thoughts that I think toward you, saith the Lord, thoughts of peace, and not of evil, to give you an unexpected end." future." God's plans for us are awesome but we need to stay on the path that God has provided. Detours cost us more than we want to give.

Macaroni and Cheese

"For God so loved the world that He gave His only begotten Son, that whoever believeth in Him shouldnot perish, but have everlasting life." John3:16 (KJV)

I have taught in several counties in North Carolina. One of the places I taught kindergarten was in Bladen County in a small rural school. I had beautiful students who were mostly African Americans. One of my favorite students' name was Billy Jack. Billy Jack was a chubby five year old who told me what he ate every meal and snack of the day.

One day Billy Jack looked at me and said, "Mrs. Rogers, me love you." I looked at Billy and said, "I love you Billy Jack!" He said, "No, Mrs. Rogers you don't understand. Me love you." I thought maybe I didn't say it with as much feeling as he did. I stoop down and looked into Billy Jack's eyes, and said, "Billy Jack, me love you too." Billy smiled and said, "Mrs. Rogers, you don't understand, me love you better than broccoli, macaroni and cheese!" Now that is true love.

Did you know that Jesus loves you better than mac and cheese? How much do you love Him?

Never Tell Dad

"Then spake Jesus again saying, I am the light of the world: he that followeth me shall not walk in darkness, but shall have the life of light." John 8:12 (KJV)

A young woman came to the crisis pregnancy center to take the volunteer training. I noticed after she took the training, she would come by the center but had a hard time staying. One day we were talking and God revealed to me that Charity had an abortion. I asked her about the abortion and she started to cry. She told me she had two abortions before she was married. Her boyfriend, later her husband, took her for the abortions. They had never talked about it. Charity had carried this guilt in her heart and soul for 10 years. Charity's Dad was a pastor and her family was pro-life. She did not want to disappoint her family. We prayed and she asked God to forgive her.

Her response was "I can never tell my Dad he will hate me." I told her I was praying for her and that she needed to tell her Dad. She left with only part of her burden lifted. Several weeks passed and Charity came back and shared that she had written her parents a letter, telling them about the abortions. She stood before them as they read the letter. They all cried and healing happened that night. Charity came by later to tell me she was sharing her story with her church family for the Sanctity of Human Life

Week. God used her story to help others make the right choice for life. Charity has healed and continues to be a voice for Life.

The Devil wants to keep us in the darkness. God wants us to come to the light so that He can be honored.

Zucchini

"A merry heart doeth good like a medicine." Proverbs 17:22a (KJV)

I have been teaching kindergarten for 38 years. One of my favorite stories is about two precious students who made my life very interesting. Their names were Ben and Wilson. I was working at a school in Rocky Mount, North Carolina. My husband was a pastor in a small church and the money I made was our main source of income. This particular year the county school system had a new evaluation system for teachers. The teacher would have a scheduled day and four evaluators would come into your room to observe you. It was my turn the next day for the evaluations.

Ben and Wilson were very energetic boys and were always into everything. My prayer for the next day was, "Dear Lord, please keep Ben and Wilson home tomorrow. You don't have to make them sick just please let them miss the bus." Guess who the first two students were to come in the next day? You guessed it, Ben and Wilson. My prayer changed, "Dear Lord, please let me keep my job." The day started and the evaluators came in with their pads and stern looks.

Our class was studying "z" words. I asked the class to give me some "z" words and they responded with words like zipper, zoo, zebra, and zoom. I asked if anyone else knew a "z" word and Wilson raised his hand. I prayed for a good answer. His answer was "zucchini". I stopped, gulped and thought "I don't know how to spell zucchini." The Lord told me to send Wilson to

God Loves You Better Than Mac And Cheese 🍪 *77*

the library with a note. Let him find the word in the dictionary and came back and write it on the board. The librarian would help him. Wilson left the class and came back bouncing into the room. He wrote the word on the board. He was so proud of himself. (I knew it was right because the librarian wrote me a note.)

I asked Wilson, "What is zucchini Wilson?" He looked at me and answered, "You didn't tell me to find out what it was, Mrs. Rogers. You only told me to write it on the board." I asked the class if they knew the meaning of zucchini. Ben raised both his hands and I knew the evaluators had seen him since he was the only one with his hands up. I looked at Ben and prayed, "Ben, what is zucchini?" He stood up and put his hands on his hips and said, "Mrs. Rogers, zucchini, that's what women wear on the beach." Needless to say the evaluators and I had a good chuckle over that answer. By the way, I got a great review that day. Oh, what I would have missed if God had answered my prayer to keep these two boys home.

The Dead Cat

"In everything give thanks: for this is the will of God in Christ Jesus concerning you."
1Thessalonians 5:18 (KJV)

My teaching career continued with Ben making my kindergarten days lively. Ben brought in many interesting show and tell items each day. His most interesting one was the day he brought in a dead cat for show and tell. Ben walked in with a big bag and I asked him what was in the bag. He said, "Mrs. Rogers I brought a dead cat for show and tell." I smiled thinking Ben was teasing me and he had a stuffed animal in the bag. I told him to put the bag on the back table.

The class started with ABC's and 123's and what is that smell? I walked over to Ben's bag and looked inside and there was a dead cat in the bag. I asked God what I should do with Ben and the dead cat. God said that I must speak life into this situation. I called all the students over and told them that Ben had a special show and tell. We did not take the cat out of the bag, I just let the students look into the bag. All the students looked, some said things like "that's gross", and "I'll give you my lunch money for the cat." The show and tell time was finished. I put the dead cat on the patio for fresh air. The day ended and I asked the Lord, "What am I suppose to do with this dead cat?" God said, "How did it get here?" I replied, "The bus, Lord." He told me to send it home on the bus. I tied up the bag and gave it to the bus driver and told her not to open the bag. I reminded her that the bag had to get off with Ben. The bus driver looked a little scared.

That night I got a call from Ben's Mom. She apologized for the dead cat. I asked her if Ben got the cat home okay. She said that the cat was home now, it had been to choir practice and boy scouts with Ben. Dad and Ben had just buried the cat in the back yard. Ben's Mom said that if I needed anything this year to please let her know. I told her I would send a list tomorrow of things needed for the classroom.

My question to you is "What do you do with the dead cats in your life?" God says that every situation should be handled with words of life.

Tim and the Tape

"Rejoice in the Lord, O ye righteous: for praise is comely for the upright." Psalm 33:1 (KJV)

Tim is my youngest son and he has a way of making others laugh. Ed, my husband, had just accepted a pastorate in a small community. The church we had just left was alive and vibrant. The church we were sent to was cold and somber. The choir would sing and they looked sad. The joy of Jesus was missing. I prayed, "Dear Lord, please touch that choir with your loving spirit. Please let them smile." Tim was sitting beside me.

I looked at the choir and they were smiling. I started praising the Lord and then I looked at Tim. He had gone into my pocketbook and taken a piece of masking tape, and put a happy smile on the tape with a marker, and placed it over his mouth. He had a pencil in his hand and he was leading the choir. I smiled at my son and told him I would give him a dollar to do that every Sunday. God can use a child to help adults remember to bring joy and honor to Him.

The Truck

"Teaching them to observe all things whatsoever I have commanded you: and, lo, I am with you always even unto the ends of the world." Matthew 28:20 (KJV)

I travel many miles a week going to these crisis pregnancy centers. I always pray for traveling mercies. One night as I was leaving the center, one of my volunteers ran over to my car. She told me that she needed to pray for my safety in going home. God had told her that the Devil wanted to destroy me for all the life work going on in the ministries. The volunteer prayed. I left the center and I was driving down a very deserted part of the highway. All of a sudden an eighteen wheeler truck was on my side coming straight at me. I cried, "Jesus, help me!" and I closed my eyes. When I looked up the truck was behind me still on my side of the road. It was as if God had carried the truck over me. I thank God every day for being my Protector.

How many times has Jesus saved you as you travel the highways of life? You will know one day when you get to heaven.

The Turkey

"For in the time of trouble he shall hide me safe in His pavilion: in the secret of his tabernacle shall he hide me; he shall set me upon a rock." Psalm 27:5 (KJV)

I had an unusual life as a child. I was the oldest of four children and I had to walk a mile to meet the school bus. The bus stop was at my Uncle Ed's house. Every morning I would walk to the bus stop afraid of the turkey at my Uncle's house. You see I had red hair and that old Tom Turkey would chase me. I would hide behind the tree and wait for the school bus. My cousin Baxter drove the school bus. He would open the doors and holler, "Run, Helen, run." I would run to the bus door with that old turkey chasing me. One day, Baxter hollered, "Run Helen Run." I ran as fast as I could but that turkey was hot on my heels. He followed me onto the school bus. I ran to the back of the bus and hid. All the students were screaming. Baxter picked up that turkey with his hands and threw him off the bus. Everybody cheered. I went straight to Uncle Ed that afternoon and told him about that mean old turkey. Uncle Ed promised that he would take care of him. I got the turkey leg at Thanksgiving and I was very happy. God answers prayers even the prayer of a six year old who is afraid of a turkey.

My Baptism

"And these things write we unto you, that your joy may be full." 1 John 1:4 (KJV)

My family went to a Methodist Church when I was growing up. I was saved and sprinkled with water when I was nine years old. Ed and I were married and we decided to join a local Baptist church. I had to be re-baptized in the Baptist church. No one knew how petrified I was of water. I almost drowned as a teenager and that caused a great fear of water. The Pastor called my name as I walked into the baptistery. Fear consumed me and I clung onto the glass sides as the pastor tried to push me down. I just knew I was going to drown. I had just married my wonderful husband and I didn't want to die yet. The pastor struggled to push me down in the water as I fought him. He said, "I baptize you in the name of the Father, Son and the Holy Spirit." Everyone in the congregation was laughing. The pastor just shook his head and gave a chuckle. He told me that I caused more joy with my baptism than he had ever seen before.

Dawn's Graduation

"Whose adorning let it not be that outward adorning of plaiting the hair, and of wearing of gold, or of putting on of apparel:." 1 Peter 3:3 (KJV)

My family has made many memories together. They say that I am the one who has made the most memories for our family. One of our funniest memories is the day that my daughter Dawn was chief Marshall at her school. I was so proud of her. I decided to buy a new dress for the occasion. I decided to go to Belk's instead of Wal-Mart since this was such a special time. I found a lovely dress with a jacket. I put the dress on and it just didn't feel right. I sat on the front row as Dawn came down the aisle. I was so proud. Dawn walked by me and whispered "Mom, you have your dress on backward." No wonder the dress didn't wear good. I smiled and said, "New style, Dawn." We have learned over the years as a family to find the joy in every situation.

Mission Home

"And the King shall answer and say unto them, Verily I say unto you, Inasmuch as ye have done it unto one of the least of these my brethren, ye have done it unto me." Matthew 25:40 (KJV)

Last November a couple called and asked if my husband and I could meet them at a home in Fayetteville. This couple showed us around the home and shared about the new roof, new siding, new windows, and other things about the home. Then she turned to us and asked us we would like this home for the ministry. We told her "yes". She handed us the keys and the deed to the home. We stood there in the yard and praised the Lord for His provision. We asked God about the home and He told us to use it for families that were homeless. Two weeks later, a lady called the ministry and asked if we would like three rooms of furniture. She was moving to Germany and needed to donate the furniture. I told her I didn't have a place to store the furniture. I saw God put His hands on his hips and say, "Helen, I just gave you a home, the furniture is for the mission home." We serve an awesome God and He does not do anything half way. The Agape Home is being used for homeless families. They can live in this home for up to one year rent free. God is always on time and He wows me every day.

Pray for Me

"Confess your faults one to another, and pray for another, that ye may be healed. The effectual fervent prayer of a righteous man availeth much." James 5:16 (KJV)

I counsel with many young women each week in these crisis pregnancy centers. Many are lonely and scared. One night I had a young woman come and in and sit down. She looked at me and said, "I heard you talk about Jesus here." I told her we were a Christian ministry and we did share the Good News of Jesus. I asked Pam who prayed for her. Her answer to me was, "No one Miss Helen, prays for me."

I prayed for her that night and she asked Jesus into her heart. I hugged her and smiled, "Pam, who is praying for you?" She smiled and said, "Miss Helen, you are praying for me." We all need prayer. Will you reach out and pray for a stranger today? God commands us to pray for each other.

The Dream

"Then saith he unto his disciples, The harvest truly is plenteous, but the labourers are few."
Matthew 9:37 (KJV)

I grew up on a farm and Daddy grew acres of cotton. I would stand in the middle of the cotton field holding Daddy's hand. If you looked at the sky, you could see that there was a terrible storm coming. The cotton needed to be picked before the rains came. I said, "Daddy, how are we ever going to get all the cotton in before the storm comes?" Daddy smiled and said, "Helen, God will provide."

We looked up and we saw all the relatives and neighbors coming down our road bringing their cotton sacks. (There were no big cotton picking machines back in those days.) Everyone worked hard and picked all day. Soon the harvest was in safe from the storms. All the friends and relatives put the food they had brought together and we had a feast. My cousins and I would played games, one of them was called, "There ain't no booger bears out tonight, Daddy killed them all last night."

We would run and chase lightning bugs and put them in Mason jars. They were our night lights. Everyone went home and the storms came. I was safe in my bed with the lightning bugs flickering. The thunder was loud and the lightning flashed and the hard rains came. As I lay there in my bed safe and dry, I could hear my Daddy's words ringing in my ear, "God will provide, Helen." God did provide and He still provides for us every day.

The other night I saw the cotton fields white unto harvest. Each cotton bole is the face of a precious baby waiting to be born. On the horizon is abortion led by the devil himself. He is coming to kill and steal. There are a few workers in the field with spectators on the sidelines. The spectators are shouting, "Save the babies!" The spectators will not leave the sidelines to help. I stand in the middle of the cotton field crying for all the precious babies that would lose their lives because Christians did nothing. For babies to die to abortion, all it takes is Christian people doing nothing. I woke up in tears. Will you help fight the battle for life?

Money Hunt

"Ask, and it shall be given to you; seek, and you will find; knock, and it shall be opened unto you." Matthew 7:7 (KJV)

My family is a spur of the moment family. One day we decided to all go to Disney World in Florida. Back then, you could take a $1000 and take a family of six for four days to Florida. Ed gave me the $1000 to keep up with and I put the money in my purse. Our family climbed in the car and we headed for Florida. We got on interstate 95 and drove to the Georgia rest stop.

    I took all the children to the bathroom and gave them a snack. I had 4 children in tow, a snack bag, and my purse. It was time to go so I placed my purse on top of the car. I put the children in their seatbelts, and put the snack bag in the bag. The motor started and we pulled out of the Georgia rest stop. Dawn said, "Mama something just fell off the top of the car." I hollered "Stop."

    Ed pulled over and we backed down the highway where the purse had fallen off. My purse was scattered all over the side of the road. There was money everywhere. I took my eight year old and six year old out of the car and told them we where going to play a game. The contest was to see who could find the most money. If we found most of it, we could go on to Florida. Marsha found a $20.00 bill and I told her that was great. Dawn picked up a $10.00 bill and threw it back down because it was not as much as a $20.00. I told her to keep the $10.00 bill and find another $10.00 and then she would have $20.00. God is so good. We picked up $990.00 off the side of the road that day and we had a great time in Florida. My children are adults now but every time we get in the car they all say, "Mom, where is your purse?" God says that we should seek and we will find. I believe that He helped us find all that money that day. We sang praises to Jesus all the way to Florida and back. We made a memory!

God is Calling

"Whosoever therefore shall humble himself as this little child, the same is the greatest in the kingdom of heaven." Matthew 18:4 (KJV)

I have been a kindergarten teacher for 38 years and everyday was an adventure. In the early years of teaching, messages from the office were delivered over the intercom. My new class had just settled in for their first day in kindergarten. Just then an announcement came over the intercom telling us what time our lunches would be. Brandon looked around, he could not figure out where the voice was coming from. Brandon said, "Mrs. Rogers, I believe God is calling you." I smiled and explained the intercom to Brandon. Children are such a blessing. They make us stop and think about the things of God. Is God calling you?

Poochie and the Snake

"Because he hath set his love upon me, therefore will I deliver him: I will set him on high, because he hath known my name." Psalm 91:14 (KJV)

I grew up on a farm with my brother and sisters. One day my Daddy drove up in the yard on the tractor and there was something poking his head out of Daddy's shirt. It was a little white puppy and I named it Poochie. Poochie and I became best friends as we roamed the farm and woods. My sisters and I liked to play house at the old tobacco barn. We headed to the barn with out tea set. Poochie was with us and started barking and growling at us. He would not let us come close to the barn. We ran to tell Daddy something was wrong. Daddy came and Poochie showed Daddy the danger. There were two poisonous snakes behind a piece of tin. Poochie saved our lives.

God says that He will protect his children with angels guarding them. I believe that God used that little white dog to save us from harm. God is a good Father.

Are You a Dandelion?

"Be still, and know that I am God: I will be exalted among the heathen, I will be exalted in the earth." Psalm 46:10 (KJV)

I walk around the walking track each morning. This morning as I was walking I noticed the little yellow dandelions sprouting up everywhere. I thought that this flower could teach us something about God. I love the yellow face on the flower. The yellow face reminds me that we should be joyful as we go through this world. Where do you find Dandelions? The answer is everywhere. You can find them on the lawns of rich people and in the weeds of the people in the projects. You can find them in beautiful flower beds and in the cracks of the sidewalks.

Have you ever tried to pull a Dandelion up from the ground? The roots seem to go to China. When the Dandelion matures, the wind scatters the seeds all around. We should be joyful as the little yellow face. Christians should be everywhere sharing the Good News of Jesus Christ. Our roots as Christians should be deep in the ground not easily removed or destroyed. We as Christians should be missionaries spreading the Word to the lost and unsaved.

I especially love a bouquet of dandelions in the hands of a child. What others see as weeds, the child sees as a beautiful flower. God sees each one of us as beautiful flowers. Take notice the next time you see a dandelion.

The Man on the Cadillac

"I therefore, the prisoner of the Lord, beseech you that ye walk worthy of the vocation wherewith ye are called, With all lowliness and meekness, with longsuffering, forbearing one another in love." Ephesians 4:1-2 (KJV)

My Dad was a farmer and times were tough on the farm when I was growing up. My little brother was born with Cystic Fibrosis. He had many health problems and the bills were staggering. Daddy was a man of faith and prayer. He prayed that God would help with all the bills. Daddy's prayers were answered because they found gravel on Daddy's land. He was paid $60,000.00 for his farm. Daddy sold the farm and purchased the old home place up the road.

Daddy always tithed no matter what the bills were. I saw Daddy write a check for $6,000 to our church. The church was trying to collect $6,000 to replace the roof of the church. That Sunday Daddy put the check in the offering plate in an envelope without putting the amount on the outside. Daddy had told me not to tell anyone that he had given the check. He said that was between God and him. He didn't want the praises of man, he wanted God's praise. Everyone was excited about the offering that Sunday. The roof was paid for but who could have put the money in the offering plate? The congregation kept asking, finally someone said, "It had to be the man on the Cadillac." Daddy only smiled and winked at me. Daddy taught me much that day. He taught me about prayer, faith and doing things for God's Glory. Thanks Dad!

Together Forever

"For our heart shall rejoice in him, because we have trusted his holy name." Psalm 33:21 (KJV)

I was blessed with a special Aunt and Uncle in my life. Aunt Elizabeth and Uncle Lynn got married later in life. They had no children of their own but loved all the nieces and nephews. Aunt Elizabeth was very close to me and my two sisters. She kept us many times for Mom and Dad to go to the hospital to stay with our little brother. Aunt Elizabeth loved us as if we were her own. Later on, we found out that Aunt Elizabeth had been married before and because of an alcoholic husband she had to put her daughters up for adoption. She missed her girls so she gave us her love. In a sense, she adopted us. Aunt Elizabeth was the best cook and Uncle Lynn gave us great rides in his old truck. Aunt Elizabeth and Uncle Lynn's love for each other was very evident. She always said that if Uncle Lynn died she was going with him. They acted like they were always on their honeymoon even after twenty-five years of marriage.

One winter, Aunt Elizabeth got very sick and had to go to the hospital. She was seriously ill. Uncle Lynn sat beside her bed holding her hand. The more critical Aunt Elizabeth became the sadder Uncle Lynn became. As Uncle Lynn was holding her hand, he had a heart attack and they rushed him to the fifth floor of the hospital. Aunt Elizabeth was on the third floor and Uncle Lynn was on the fifth floor of the same hospital. I came home from the hospital and prayed that God's will would be done.

I got two phone calls from the hospital that night. The first call said that Aunt Elizabeth had died. The second call said that Uncle Lynn had died five minutes later. I could not cry for them. They loved each other in life and God had blessed them to go together in death. They walked hand in hand into heaven together never to be separated again. It was a beautiful funeral, a memorial to a couple who loved God, loved each other and loved all they met.

A Blessing

"For great is the Lord, and greatly to be praised; he also is to be feared above all gods."
1 Chronicles 16:25 (KJV)

The pregnancy ministries are full time. At the present time we are in five counties in North Carolina. It takes many donations to keep the doors of these ministries open. We do not take any money from the government because we say the name of "Jesus" with all who enter our doors. Christian individuals and churches support us with monetary and clothing donations. One of the pregnancy ministries was in need. It did not take in enough money to pay the bills for the month. I was praying and I asked God if we should keep the ministry open since there were not enough funds. God reminded me that He is the provider of all we need. He told me to be "faithful" that was my job. God told me that there would be a blessing at the Agape Center that night. I thanked Him and headed for Fayetteville.

That night a young soldier and his family came to the center. They brought diapers, clothes, and other baby items. I thanked them and they started to leave. The young man handed me a folded piece of paper. They left and I opened the paper to find a check. The check was for

$10,000.00. I started crying and I ran through the center praising my Lord. Needless to say I am not asking God anymore about the finances of the centers. That is His part. My part is to be faithful. Thank you Jesus!

Tommy

"Wait for the Lord, be of good courage, and he shall strengthen thine heart: wait, I say, on the Lord." Psalm 27:14 (KJV)

I was the oldest of four children. Our family had three girls and one boy. My little brother Tommy was born with Cystic Fibrosis. Tommy was "red-haired" with blue eyes. He was the joy of our family. Tommy had to sleep in an oxygen tent each night and special foods had to be prepared for him. His medicine was so expensive and there was no help from others. Daddy had to leave the farm and work in public work to pay the bills. We loved Tommy and he loved us. When I would go out on a date, Tommy would stand in a chair and help me put my coat on. He would look at my date and say, "You had better take care of my sister or you will have to deal with me." Tommy was in the hospital much of his life. His last time in the hospital was just before his eighth birthday. He had been in there for a month. I was allowed to visit Tommy at Duke Hospital. His birthday was in one week. Tommy said, "Helen, Jesus came to see me last night. He told me I was going to have my birthday party with him."

Later on that night Tommy went home to heaven. Mama and Daddy said that when Tommy died the hospital room became very bright. Tommy lifted his hands and said, "Hi, Jesus, I have been waiting for you!" It was a hard time for our family but we knew that we would see him again. God has made that promise and God keeps all His promises.

Neal

"Be not forgetful to entertain strangers; for thereby some have entertained angels unawares."
Hebrews 13:2 (KJV)

Ed and I got married and we moved to Roxboro. Ed was a teacher at the local high school and I worked as a librarian assistant at an elementary school. The school I was at had many needy children. We had been married for two months when I called Ed at school and asked him if he wanted to be a father. There was a little boy named Neal that needed a home because of the arrest of his parents for drugs. Ed hesitated and said, "Yes, some day Helen. Did you forget to tell me something?" I told him about Neal and we decided to take him into our home. The first year of our marriage was very exciting as we tried to raise a six year old boy. Neal stayed with us for a year. He taught us much. We haven't seen him in forty-two years. We still pray for him. We have had four foster children in our home. Each one of them was a blessing. If God asked you to do something, don't hesitate, you might miss a blessing if you do.

The Doughnut Prayer

"Delight thyself also in the Lord; and he shall give thee the desires of thine heart."
Psalms 37:4 (KJV)

The youth group at our church had decided to sell doughnuts one very hot day in July. We went to the local Food Lion parking lot. It was so hot! I was drenched with sweat. I walked over to the sidewalk and looked up into the sky. There was not a cloud in the sky. I lifted my hands and prayed, "Dear God, please send a cool rain. It is so hot." There was a man sitting on the bench watching me. He chuckled to himself. Just then, there was a small cloud in the sky. Then came a downpour of cool refreshing rain. I said, "Thank you God!" The man looked puzzled, shook his head and moved to the other side of the parking lot. That night the weatherman reported that there was an unexpected rain shower over the Pittsboro area. I smiled, nothing is impossible for my God.

I Aborted Three Children

"And he that sat upon the throne said, Behold, I make all things new. And he said unto me, Write: for these words are true and faithful" Revelation 21:5 (KJV)

Let's meet Ginger. Ginger is a young mother with three children. She was the youth leader in her church and helped with the mission groups. One night after she went to bed, the enemy showed us and reminded her of the three abortions she had before she was married. He said, "You murdered three of your children. How can you be a good Mom to your living girls. What right do you have to teach the youth and children at church? You are not fit!" The enemy came as the accuser of her soul. She called the pregnancy center and asked if she could make an appointment to come in. She needed to talk to someone as soon as possible. I met her at thecenter the following week. She was a broken woman. She had tried to commit suicide three times in two weeks by overdosing on pills, cutting her wrists, and trying to pull her car in front of a truck. We sat and talked. She cried, "Miss Helen, I killed my babies, my babies will hate me when I get to heaven." I assured her that in heaven there is no hate. Her children will meet her at the gate of heaven and she will hear, "Oh Mommy, we love and we have missed you! Let's walk the streets of heaven together." We talked of God's love and His forgiveness. I encouraged her to name her children and then write a personal letter telling them she was sorry and that she loved them. God did a healing in her that day. We prayed and she accepted God's love and forgiveness. She also forgave herself. We did a Bible study together and she decided that God wanted her to tell her story so that other young women would chose life instead of death for their children. Today she is walking in the Light and the Devil has no more hold over her. We know that the Devil is a liar and an accuser. He comes only to rob, steal and to destroy God's most precious creation. God is truth and a deliverer. He comes to love, forgive, and to restore.

The Atheist

"The law of the Lord is prefect, converting the soul: the testimony of the Lord is sure, making wise the simple." Psalm 19: 7 (KJV)

My son and I went to a local music shop. Tim found the music he wanted. We went to the checkout and there was a young man named Rodney. I asked him if he knew Jesus as his Lord and Savior. He got angry. He said, "Why do you Christians always push this Jesus stuff? I don't know Jesus and I don't need Him." I told him that Jesus loved him and died for him. I told him I would be praying for him. His reply was, "I don't want your prayers!" I smiled and said, "You can't control my praying for you." I left that day with a prayer in my heart for this very lost young man. Later Tim and I went back to the same store. Rodney saw us coming and hid under the counter. I leaned over the counter and told him that I was still praying for him. I don't know what happened to that young man but I'm still praying for him. I believe atheists are seekers and that they have a Jesus-shaped void in their hearts. Jesus is the only one who can give value to our lives. Everyone needs Jesus. We need to share Jesus that is the great commission.

The Homeless

"And the King shall answer and say unto them, Verily I say unto you, Inasmuch as ye have done it unto one of the least of these my brethren, ye have done it unto me.." Matthew 25:40 (KJV)

The economy is bad with many Moms and families out of work. I meet many homeless Moms and children working at the crisis pregnancy center. There are just not enough resources for all the needs. I had several calls one week from homeless Moms begging for help. One mother had twin infants and a three year old and they were living in a car. I had no place to send them. On my way home from Clinton, I started talking to God. "God, where are the people you have called to start this homeless ministry for Moms and babies?" God listened and then he answered with "I have called someone and I choose you." I was speechless as I was already busy in five counties in crisis pregnancy centers. I reminded the Lord that I didn't have the time, money or land. God said, "I will make the time, I own all the land and I own the cattle on a thousand hills and the hills. I am the King with unlimited resources. I need a willing servant." My reply was "Show me Lord what I need to know."

God showed me a vision of seven small cottages in a semi-circle. The cottages are beautiful with flowers lining the walkway. There is a bigger building in the middle where the caregiver will stay with his family. The building will have a recreation room and a chapel. Part of the building can be used to take classes or for kids to study. The children's playground is Noah's Ark. This special place will be called Agape Court. It will be a place for single Moms and their children. They will be able to stay for up to a year as they work to get on their feet. God showed me this in a vision. I asked God, "Would you please tell Ed about this vision. He is already so busy helping with the crisis centers. I hurried in the house and found Ed in tears in his chair. I said, "Ed, do you know what God has been talking to me about all the way home?" He looked at me and said God has already told me and the answer is the homeless. Since then we are praying and seeking God's direction. We have been offered some land and we have a steering committee. God does not always call the most equipped but he calls those who are faithful. Pray as we undertake this adventure with our Lord.

Daddy and Me

"Thy faith hath saved thee; go in peace." Luke 7:50 (KJV)

I was blessed with Godly parents. My Daddy was an encourager and worked hard for his family. He was a farmer until my little brother was born with serious health problems. Daddy had to leave the farm to go to public work. Daddy would work from seven to three each day. I wanted to play basketball but I was not very good at it. My Daddy would sit in the parking lot for two hours while I practiced basketball. He did that for four years. Dad never complained and always encouraged me to do my best. In the four years I was on the team I made only two points. Daddy told me he was proud of me. He even had to borrow the money to buy my converse ball shoes. He never said, "give up" or "you're wasting your time and mine." His words to me were "Always do your best. I love you Helen. Do everything for Jesus!"

Ms. Halley

"I love them that love me; and those that seek me early shall find me." Proverbs 8:17 (KJV)

I have had many principals as I have taught in North Carolina for 38 years. God sent me to a school where the principal was not a Christian. It was hard working for a principal that felt that I should keep my faith to myself. Many times she would call me to the office and say, "Helen, I like your teaching but can't you keep quiet about this Jesus."I said, "Mrs. Halley, you don't know Jesus as your Lord and Savior, do you?" Her answer was "NO!' I stayed with that school for four years with always the same question, " Can't you keep quiet about this Jesus?"As the four years ended, I gave Mrs. Halley a bouquet of flowers. She smiled at me and said she was glad that she didn't change me. I told Mrs. Halley I would be praying that she would come to know Jesus. I also asked her to call me when she found Jesus. She smiled and I left with a prayer in my heart.

Four years later at 11:00 at night I received a call from Mrs. Halley. She was excited! She told me that she had asked Jesus into her heart and so had her 84 year old Mother. They were both to get baptized the next Sunday. Mrs. Halley said, "Helen, I can't be quiet about Jesus. I have called everyone that I have ever worked with and I share Jesus with all that I meet. I now understand your passion for Jesus." The following week Mrs. Halley and her mother were baptized and a month later her Mother died. Mrs. Halley now teaches a Sunday School class and she loves Jesus. It is important that we as Christians should always be bold and stand for Jesus. Your stand will never be in vain.

Bill

"A word fitly spoken is like apples of gold in pictures of silver." Proverbs 25:11 (KJV)

God has blessed me with many special children over the 38 years of teaching kindergarten. One of my favorite students was named Bill. Bill came to me with special needs. He had spinal bifida and could not walk. He was a very bright young man. The school lunchroom was 30 steps down to the school basement. Every day I would pick Bill up and carry him to the lunchroom. Each time, I would pick Bill up I would say, "Bill, God made you special. I am praying that you will walk some day." He stayed with me for two years in kindergarten. I loved Bill, he blessed me everyday with his strong will and determination.

Life goes on. I prayed for Bill even though I didn't see him. My family and I went back to visit the area. I pumped my gas and walked into the store to pay my bill. There was Bill working in the store and he was walking. He walked over and hugged me. I asked him how he was doing. He said, "Mrs. Rogers, I remember you telling me that God had a plan for me and that you were praying that I would walk. I got into a lot of trouble in high school with drugs and alcohol. I even thought that I didn't want to live. I met a Christian girl who introduced me to Jesus. We got married. We wanted children, but the doctors said, we were not able to have children. God is good, we have two beautiful children. He has blessed me." I left knowing that God answers prayers. Sometimes it takes a season of time but God is always faithful. Love given to a child is never wasted.

"Modern Day" Proverbs Women

"Many daughters have done virtuously, but thou excellest them all."
Proverbs 31:29 (KJV)

I love the scripture of the Proverbs 31 woman. I re-wrote it for the modern day woman. A wife of unique character who can find? She is worth far more that stocks and IRA's. Her husband wanders about her sanity and still smiles. She brings him laughter and joy all the days of his life. She buys Wal-Mart specials and clips coupons to save every cent she can. She is like a merchant ship bringing her food from McDonalds' and KFC. She gets up while it is dark to pack lunches and lay out clothes for her family for the day. She considers a yard sale and buys unique stuff. Out of her money she gives each child their allowance and gives the rest to someone in need. She is a taxi-driver, getting each and everyone of her children to the ball practices, dance recitals, and church functions while still keeping up with all the housework, cooking, cleaning, and shopping.

She sets about her work tired from the day before. Her heart aches for the wayward child as her knees bends many times to petition God for the needs of her family. She knows a good deal at the local store and will be there two hours early before it is gone. Her light is the last to go out at night as she has checked the doors, checked the stove and the heat. She goes into her children's room to make sure all is well. Her last stop is the Bible to read and pray for God's protection on her family. She praises God for all His blessings. In her hand she holds a list of things to be done, with a small child pulling at her leg to let's go outside and pick dandelions. She gives all her birthday money to a child in need and stretches out her heart and home to the hurting.

When it snows, she clothes her children in warm coats, scarves, and mittens and starts a snowball fight. Later she will make snow cream with them as they laugh and remember their snowy day. She has happy face pillows and sheets. Her husband is pitied at the local diner where he goes to get a cup of coffee as he shares his wife's latest adventures. She makes cookbooks and sells them to fund her kindergarten beach trip. She is clothed in clown suits, den mother outfits, hand-me-down clothes and lots of love. She smiles at the day's end asking God to forgive her for the things she didn't get done.

She speaks with Motherly authority, mostly "Do it because I said so!"She vacuums the floors, washes mountains of clothes, feeds the endless pits of hunger, does mission work and often forgets to eat herself. Her children rise up and call her again, again, and again! Her husband calls her too. Have you seen my car keys, my reading book, my glasses? I left that important paper on the dining room table two weeks ago. Did you move it? Many women work two jobs, but you have three. Charm is not on your list. Beauty is not found in jars of makeup. A woman who loves her husband and her children will leave a legacy that will stand the test of time."A hundred years from now, it will not matter how clean my house was or if all the laundry was done. What will be important is that I gave my husband and children- love, laughter, happy memories and a firm foundation in the Lord. My gift I gave them was the legacy of Jesus."

The Job

"Rejoice in the Lord, O ye righteous; for praise is comely for the upright."
Psalm 33:1 (KJV)

Ed accepted the call to the ministry after we had been married for eleven years. He accepted a church about three hours from our hometown. I had to leave the teaching job where I had been for my teaching career. I resigned with no job in hand and left for our new location. Everyone said I would "not" be able to find a teaching job. I believed God. I prayed for a kindergarten position where His name would be honored. I started looking and visiting schools. I went to a school in Rocky Mount and applied. The principal offered me a second grade position. I told him I would take the second grade until the kindergarten class was available. He looked at me and said, "Mrs. Rogers, you don't understand, there is no kindergarten position. All of my kindergarten teachers have signed their contracts and school starts next week." I smiled and said, "Just remember me when the kindergarten position is ready. I have asked God for a kindergarten class."

It was 11:00 at night and the next day was the first day of school. I received a call from the principal. He said, "Mrs. Rogers, one of my kindergarten teachers has just resigned and I believe that I am to offer you the kindergarten position." I shouted, "Praise the Lord!" God had answered my prayer when it seemed to be an impossible one. Faith walking in this life is the best exercise for the heart. God always shows up!

Mom

"Give her of the fruit of her hands; and let her own works praise her in the gates."
Proverbs 31:31 (KJV)

I was thinking of my Mom today. She died seven years ago. Here is a letter that I wrote to read at my Mom's funeral. Mama was a special lady. She never finished school and never went to college. She never won any awards. By the world's standards, she was not successful. Her greatest mission was to raise and care for her family. She cooked endless meals and washed mountains of clothes. She took care of you when you were sick and spanked you when you were unruly. Her fiery temper and red hair made you stop and take notice. The maddest she got was when you were messing with her family, especially her grandchildren. Her happiest times were Sunday dinners with the house full of family usually with great-grandchildren on her lap.

She cared for many children in the nursery at the church and in our home. All the kids knew Miss Mary and she was as proud of them as her own. All our lives God and church were placed first in our home. Mama loved going to church with Daddy and us kids. She was proud of her family. She fought hard to stay here on Earth even though there were many in heaven waiting for her. She only thought about letting go of earth when she no longer was able to care for the family she loved. Thank you Mama for being there for us. There was no substitute for your love. Your love showed us Jesus from the time we were born. We were your mission field. You sang Jesus loves me and read Bible stories to us. You made every holiday special and made our home warm and happy. You see Mama accepted the greatest calling that a woman can have and that was the name of wife and Mother. Mama, we love you, you gave us Jesus.

Math Teacher of the Year

"But seek ye first the kingdom of God, and his righteousness: and all these things shall be added unto you." Matthew 6:33 (KJV)

I was an average student in school. I worked hard for B's and C's. Learning didn't come easily especially Math. It was my hardest subject and I struggled through all the math courses. I told God that when I became a teacher I was going to try to find ways to make math easier especially for the struggling students. I became a kindergarten teacher and I taught math with lots of hands on activities. I measured the students to sunflowers and penguins. One of the math activities was to see how many kindergarten feet would fit inside of Tyrannosaurus Rex's footprint. Paper plate faces had to have 10 chicken pox. I would make a picnic basket and the ants would come to the basket by 2's, 5's and 10's. I was enjoying Math and the students were learning. My principal came by and told me that he had nominated me for Math Teacher of the Year from our school. I smiled and thought my God certainly has a sense of humor. What was even funnier was that I won Teacher of the Year for the county. I had to go to Charlotte to a reception honoring all the county winners. I received a gold medal. This Kindergarten teacher was sitting with Calculus and Math geniuses. My God truly has a sense of humor. He can take our weaknesses and make them into strengths if we commit everything to Him. I have that gold medal on my wall at home to remind me that nothing is impossible for God.

Jesus With Skin On

"But the path of the just is as the shinning light, that shineth more and more unto the perfect day." Proverbs 4:18 (KJV)

I was pregnant, scared and alone

And you gossiped about me and discussed my predicament.

I was kicked out of my home when my parents found out I was pregnant.

You looked away and said I could get welfare.

I had no clothes for my new baby,

You said I was an unfit Mother.

I wanted to give my baby life but

There was no one to show me how.

I was lonely and you turned your back on me and pointed out my sins.

I needed Jesus and you were afraid to tell me about Him.

You seem so close to God,

But I'm still pregnant, scared and alone!

What will I do?

I feel so trapped, I wanted more for my baby than what I had.

If I abort, my child will not have to go through the pain and hurt of this life.

Does anyone care?

Yes, my child, I care.

I will care with God's love.I will love you, pray for you and help you.

I have clothes for your baby.

I will mentor you and teach you how to be a good Mom.

Most of all, I would like to introduce you to Jesus.

You see Jesus loves you and your baby.

He has plans for you both.

I will be the hands, the feet, and the heart of Jesus.

Jesus is your only hope!

I Needed A Dad

"And when he was gone forth into the way, there came one running, and kneeled to him and asked him, Good Master, what shall I do that I may inherit eternal life?" Mark 10: 17 (KJV)

I see many women working in crisis pregnancy centers but I also get an opportunity to share Jesus with the fathers of the babies. One night I was volunteering at the center in Lumberton when a young couple came in. She was pregnant and due within the month. You could tell the young man was there very reluctantly. I counseled with the young woman and asked what she needed for the baby. I asked about her relationship with Jesus. She said that she did not know Jesus. I shared God's love with her. I told her of a Savior who had died for her sins and asked her if she would like to accept Jesus. She said, "Yes!" I turned to the young man and asked him about Jesus. He told me that he had no use for Jesus. The conversation turned to his life. I asked him about his relationship with his father. Was his father there for him? Did he take him to church and to ballgames? Could you talk to your father? Did he ever tell you, he loved you? I also asked if his life would have been different if his Dad had been there for him. He had tears in his eyes and said he always wanted a Dad that loved him and cared for him. I turned to his girlfriend and pointed to her womb and said, "You have a son that will soon be here, don't you want better for him?" You can be the Dad that you always wanted to be for your son. His answer was, "I want to ask Jesus into my life. I want to be a good Dad." That night that precious little one got two parents that accepted Jesus. I then asked, "How many years have you lived together?" He told me that they had been living together for three years. I said, "Isn't it time for you two to make it right before the Lord." They both agreed and will be married within the month.

Author

My name is Helen McLeod Rogers. I live in Fayetteville, North Carolina. I have been married to Rev. Ed Rogers for 42 years. We have six children and 5 precious grandchildren. I have been a kindergarten teacher for 38 years in North Carolina. I have a Master's Degree in Early Childhood. Twenty four years ago I took a stand for Life. Since that time my husband and I have started 12 crisis pregnancy centers in North Carolina. I am at present the Director of five pregnancy centers in 5 counties in North Carolina. God Loves You Better Than Mac and Cheese is a result of the many miracles I have seen in these ministries. I serve an awesome God and these stories show His greatness.

If you would like to tell stories that show that God Loves You Better Than Mac and Cheese, please e-mail me at wrogers15@nc.rr.com.

CPSIA information can be obtained at www.ICGtesting.com
Printed in the USA
BVOW03s2041270414

351748BV00002B/4/P